The Real Patriots of the American Revolution

The Real Patriots of the American Revolution

★ ★ ★

BY ROBERT YOUNG

DILLON PRESS
Parsippany, New Jersey

For
Bill Bigelow, Roscoe Caron, Larry Lewin,
and the many teachers
who encourage their students to think

Acknowledgments

I am grateful to Randall McGowen for providing an important clarification, to Debbie Biber for her patient editorial support, and to my family for their continued encouragement.

Photo Credits

Cover: Library of Congress.

Archive Photos: 28 *t.* The Granger Collection, New York: 10 *b.*, 65. Library of Congress: 2, 6, 8, 14, 16, 17, 19, 21, 24, 28 *b.*, 29, 32, 33, 36, 38, 39, 41, 44, 45, 47, 51, 53, 55, 56, 60, 67, 69. North Wind Picture Archives: 10 *t.*, 66.

Library of Congress Cataloging-in-Publication Data

Young, Robert, 1951–
    The real patriots of the American Revolution/by Robert Young.—1st ed.
      p. cm.—(Both Sides)
    Includes bibliographical references and index.
    ISBN 0-87518-612-2 (LSB).—ISBN 0-382-39171-3 (pbk.)
    1. United States—History—Revolution, 1775-1783—Juvenile literature. 2. Revolutionaries—United States—History—18th century—Juvenile literature. 3. American loyalists—Juvenile literature. I. Title II. Series: Both Sides (Dillon Press)
    E208.Y7   1996
    973.3—dc20   95-35510

Summary: An examination of who were the real patriots during the American Revolution—those who fought for freedom and independence or those who loyally supported Great Britain.

 Published by Dillon Press
A Division of Simon & Schuster
299 Jefferson Road, Parsippany, NJ 07054

First edition

Printed in the United States of America

10 9 8 7 6 5 4 3 2 1

★ ★ ★ Contents ★ ★ ★

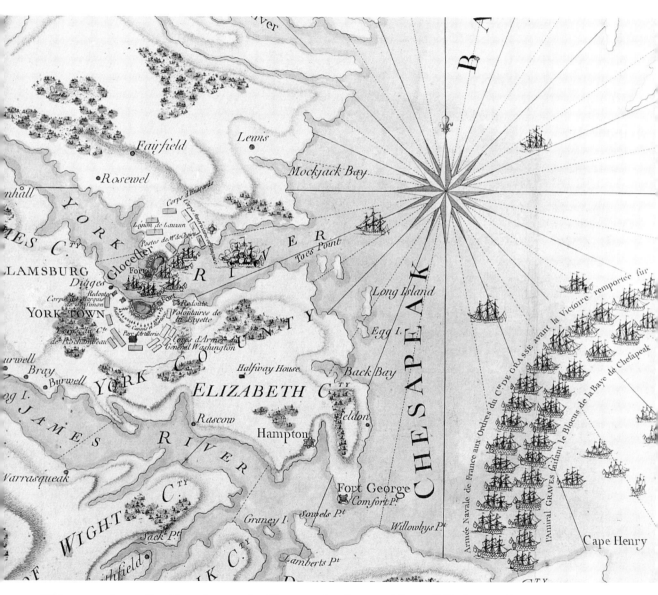

This map shows the French navy in Chesapeake Bay, cutting off Yorktown by sea and thereby trapping Cornwallis and his British troops.

ONE

The Surrender

The Revolutionary War was nearing an end on September 28, 1781, when 8,845 American soldiers joined nearly 8,000 French troops and 30 French warships in cutting off Yorktown by land and sea. Facing the American and French troops on that peninsula in Virginia were about 7,000 soldiers under British command. Some were German soldiers, called Hessians, who had been hired by the British. Others were Americans, called Loyalists or Tories, who were supporting Great Britain. Most of the soldiers were British.

For days the Americans, under the command of General George Washington, and the French, under the command of the Count de Rochambeau, had dug trenches and placed their cannons and mortar into position. On the morning of October 9, Washington fired the first cannon to begin the siege of Yorktown. According to a witness, Washington's first shot smashed into a house where British officers

The only chance for the British to win at Yorktown was to get reinforcements. When Sir Henry Clinton, who commanded a force of British soldiers in New York, learned about the situation at Yorktown, he frantically worked to send help. But the British had a shortage of materials, and their ships needed repair. It wasn't until October 17 that his 7,000 soldiers sailed south for Yorktown.

were eating dinner. The shot hit the officer sitting at the head of the table.

During the first day of fighting, the Americans and the French fired 3,600 cannon and mortar shots into enemy lines. The next day firing continued for hours on end. Lord Charles Cornwallis, who commanded the British, Loyalists, and Hessians, knew that his troops could not last much longer against these attacks. Food was getting scarce, disease was

Lord Charles Cornwallis

on the rise, and the soldiers were trapped on a peninsula with little chance for victory.

There was a chance for escape, though. Cornwallis drew up a plan to take his army across the York River to Gloucester Point. From there they would march north through Virginia, Maryland, and Pennsylvania to join other British forces.

As the Americans and French troops advanced, Cornwallis began his daring escape. The first wave of boats carrying his troops reached Gloucester successfully. But that night a storm blew in, scattering the boats and ending all hopes for further escape.

Early on the morning of October 17, American and French troops continued to batter the British lines with cannon and mortar fire. And then about ten o'clock, as the soldiers shifted their weapons into new positions, a small red-coated figure walked out from behind one of the British earthworks. It was a drummer boy, and he was pounding a message on his drum. The message was that the British wanted to meet with the Americans and the French. Following the boy was a British officer waving a white handkerchief.

The battlefield became quiet as the two figures slowly walked forward through the haze of drifting gun smoke. One of Washington's staff officers ran out to meet them. He sent the drummer boy back to his lines and then blindfolded the officer and led him to

A British drummer boy and an officer approach American lines asking for a truce.

the Americans' field headquarters. The officer was carrying a sealed letter, which was taken to General Washington at nearby Williamsburg. It read:

> *I propose a cessation of hostilities for twenty-four hours, and that two officers may be appointed by each side to meet at Mr. Moore's house to settle terms for the surrender of the posts of York and Gloucester. I have the honor to be,*
>
> Sir,
>
> *your most obedient and humble servant,*
> *Cornwallis*

Washington was pleased but cautious. Thinking Cornwallis was stalling for time to get help, Washington gave him only two hours to submit his surrender proposal.

Talks and planning between the two sides continued for another day. And then on October 19, 1781, the surrender ceremony took place. That afternoon the troops under the command of Cornwallis, with drums beating and music playing, marched onto the field of surrender. Because Cornwallis claimed to be sick, the troops were led by Brigadier General Charles O'Hara, second in command.

When O'Hara offered his sword as a symbol of surrender to the French commander, Rochambeau waved him toward Washington. O'Hara then offered the sword to Washington, but he would not take it either. It was not proper for a commander to accept surrender from the second in command. Washington

★ ★ ★ ★ ★ ★ ★ ★ ★ ★ ★ ★ ★

In his terms for surrender, Cornwallis asked that his men be allowed to return to their homes in Europe under the condition that they would not fight against America or France. Washington, remembering the unconditional surrender the British demanded when the Americans surrendered at Charleston, refused.

Cornwallis asked that Loyalists and American army deserters who had helped the British not be punished. Washington again refused, but he agreed to allow one ship to sail to New York. That ship carried Americans who had strongly supported the British and who would probably be the most harshly punished if they were caught.

then directed O'Hara to Major General Benjamin Lincoln, who accepted the sword for the Americans and the French.

The British troops marched between lines of American and French soldiers to another field. There they surrendered their weapons. Some laid their guns down sadly; others threw them down angrily. By the end of the day, the American and French troops had seized thousands of guns and 250 pieces of artillery as well as equipment and supplies. They also had captured 7,247 British, Loyalist, and Hessian soldiers and 840 seamen.

The British surrender at Yorktown was a tremendous victory for the Americans and the French. But more than that, history shows that this was the last major battle of the Revolutionary War, a war that had pitted the American colonists and later the French against the British and against themselves.

Who were the real patriots—people who love and defend their country—in this war? Were they the people who opposed British rule and favored a new and independent nation? Or were they the people who remained loyal and continued to support Great Britain? This book will examine both sides of the issue and encourage you to decide for yourself.

TWO

Sons of Liberty

Many people believe that the American colonists who called themselves Patriots had good reason to do so. They also believe that the Patriots had good reason to fight for independence against Great Britain. To better understand this viewpoint, it is important to review some colonial history.

During the seventeenth and early eighteenth centuries, England, France, and Spain—the three great European powers—were all trying to control the lands of the North American continent. By the middle of the 1700s, Great Britain possessed a row of thirteen colonies that stretched along the Atlantic coast.

Each of the colonies was linked with the mother country by a charter, a document that listed the colonists' rights and privileges. The main governing group in each colony was the assembly, or legislature, made up of locally elected men. However, any laws passed by the assembly had to be sent to Great

Britain and approved by representatives of the king.

Most of the colonies had governors who were appointed or approved by the king. Often the governor was appointed as a reward for special service in Great Britain, not necessarily because he was a capable leader. Many did not understand America or its people and made little effort to learn. Given the governors' ignorance as well as the colonists' interest in protecting their rights, conflicts were bound to arise.

King George III

In 1760, at age 22, George III became king of Great Britain. At that time the British were fighting for territory in North America against the French and some Native Americans. With the help of the colonists, the British won the French and Indian War in 1763, which added more land for their colonies. But the war had been very expensive, complained British leaders, so the colonists should have to help pay for it, even though they had fought, too.

Despite the opposing arguments, Parliament, the lawmaking body of Great Britain, passed the Sugar Act in 1764. This law taxed certain products, restricted the trading of others, and made it easier for customs officials to enforce the trade laws.

Next came the Stamp Act, which required colonists to pay a tax on publications, legal documents, licenses, and even playing cards! The tax was to be paid by buying a stamp and putting it on

The Sugar Act actually served to help colonists organize against the British. When members of the Massachusetts legislature learned of the new taxes, it appointed a committee to correspond, or communicate by letter, to other colonies. In time, more of these groups, called committees of correspondence, were created, making a network throughout the colonies. These committees were very helpful in quickly reporting important information to help the cause of the Patriots.

each of the taxed items. The cost of the stamps would vary according to the cost of the items on which they would be placed. Colonists were told that the money raised from these taxes would be used to help pay for the British army that defended them. The colonists were also ordered to provide barracks and supplies for the troops.

The colonists were not happy when they heard about the Stamp Act. Times were hard, and many people did not have the extra money to pay the tax. They were also angry because they had no part in making the decision to tax. The colonists were not against paying for their defense, but they suggested that the assembly in each colony be asked to contribute voluntarily. They argued that Parliament had no right to impose taxes on them. Only their own elected government should be able to do that.

The Stamp Act further united the colonists who were opposed to British rule and willing to fight for independence from their mother country. They became known as Patriots. To fight the Stamp Act,

Patriots organized themselves into groups called the Sons of Liberty. Members of the Sons of Liberty did what they could to influence others against the unfair tax. They wrote letters, made speeches, and organized protests. At times they put pressure on the tax collectors to resign.

Patrick Henry, a Patriot and a member of Virginia's assembly called the House of Burgesses, introduced a set of resolutions on May 29, 1765. In them he stated that the state's charter gave Virginians the

Colonists protesting the Stamp Act

16

same rights as the British, and that one of those rights was the right to be taxed by people they had elected to represent them. Only the Virginia assembly had the right to tax Virginians.

These resolutions, known as the Virginia Resolves, were printed and sent to other colonies. Many other Patriots supported Henry. In Massachusetts

Patrick Henry was a powerful orator.

the legislature called for a congress of colonial leaders to consider unified action against Great Britain.

The response was encouraging. Representatives from nine of the 13 colonies met in New York City in October 1765. After much debate the delegates created a Declaration of Rights and Grievances, which stated that there should be "no taxation without representation." This important meeting was the first time the colonies had come together for a common purpose.

The result of the colonists' efforts was positive. Within a year of passing the Stamp Act, Parliament repealed, or canceled, it. But along with the good news of the repeal came bad news. Parliament made it clear that it still had the right to tax the colonies.

It wasn't long before the British again demonstrated their right to tax the colonies. In 1767, Parliament passed the Townshend Acts, named after

★ ★ ★ ★ ★ ★ ★ ★ ★ ★ ★ ★ ★ ★ ★

A strong voice in the fight against the Stamp Act was Samuel Adams, a Massachusetts businessman and organizer of the Sons of Liberty. Adams came from a wealthy family and knew firsthand the power and unfairness of the British government. In the 1740s, Sam's father had founded a bank called the Land Bank in Boston. He had used his money as well as contributions from 800 merchants to start the bank. But Parliament disapproved of the Land Bank, and they voted to close it. All the investors lost their money, and Sam's father's fortune was nearly wiped out.

Charles Townshend, chancellor of the exchequer. These laws required colonists to pay taxes on imported goods such as glass, lead, paint, paper, and tea. The law also gave British officials the right to inspect ships, businesses, and even homes to make sure the taxes were being paid.

Sam Adams

The Townshend Acts did more than add another tax to the colonies. It took away New York's right to have an elected government for refusing to pay to keep British soldiers in New York City. To New Yorkers, it wasn't fair that they should have to pay the entire cost of the soldiers who were protecting all the colonies. When New York finally paid, its assembly was able to meet, but many colonists did not forget the harsh action of Great Britain.

The taxes brought about by the Townshend Acts were continued examples of taxation without representation. Again, Patriots fought back. In Massachusetts, Patriots organized a boycott that included not only the taxed products but all British goods. They were determined to send a strong message to the British.

The British, however, were not listening. Instead, they used more force to strengthen their hold over the colonies. In June 1768, British officials seized the ship of John Hancock, a well-known Patriot leader. When colonists protested, British officials requested more troops to keep order.

King George sent 4,000 more British soldiers to Massachusetts.

The presence of additional troops did not bring about peace. The troops served as daily reminders of an unjust country imposing its will on the colonists and of declining freedoms in the colonies. As a result, protests continued, and fights broke out between colonists and British soldiers, who were called redcoats or lobsterbacks because of the color of their uniforms.

The next year Colonel George Washington of the Virginia House of Burgesses introduced another set of resolves. In them Washington criticized Great Britain for its treatment of the Massachusetts colony and warned the British against threats of further action. After the resolves received unanimous support from the legislature, Virginia's royal governor declared they could no longer meet. But that did not stop the representatives. They moved to a nearby tavern to conduct their business, and they continued to work for colonial unity.

The following year things got worse. On the evening of March 5, 1770, British soldiers fired into a group of Boston citizens, killing five. It was a massacre, charged Sam Adams, and it showed that having an army around during peacetime was a threat to liberty. Adams urged the colonists to declare their independence from Great Britain. Silversmith

Paul Revere's engraving of the Boston Massacre

Paul Revere made an engraving of the Boston Massacre and distributed it to help communicate what had happened.

Frustrated at its attempts to raise money in America, Parliament decided to repeal the Townshend Acts, except for the small tax on tea. This tax was continued to show colonists that Parliament still had the right to tax them.

In 1773, Parliament passed the Tea Act to help the struggling British East India Company. The act allowed the company to ship its tea directly to America, avoiding import duties in Great Britain. It also gave the British East India Company a monopoly of the tea trade in the colonies.

Seeing that colonial merchants were at the total mercy of British officials, the Patriots had no choice but to protest this action. When East India ships began to arrive in Boston ports, the Sons of

Liberty refused to allow them to unload the tea. The ships' captains matched this response by refusing to leave the harbor as ships in other cities had done. Boston Harbor became the sight of a showdown. Then on the night of December 16, a number of men dressed up as Mohawks boarded three ships and dumped 342 chests, containing 35,000 pounds of tea, into Boston Harbor.

British officials acted quickly when they heard the news of the Boston Tea Party. They passed a series of laws called the Intolerable Acts to punish Massachusetts. They hoped that punishing Massachusetts so severely would accomplish two things. One was to frighten other colonists into accepting British control. The other was for the other colonists to take advantage of the misfortune of Massachusetts. Since ships were not allowed to enter the port of Boston, other cities such as New York, Philadelphia, and Baltimore could benefit by having the ships come into their ports.

The British, however, were not aware of the growing unity in the colonies. Instead of taking advantage of Massachusetts's problems, people in surrounding colonies sent food, clothing, and money to Massachusetts. Instead of fearing the British, they resented the growing interference.

In June 1774, leaders in Massachusetts called for another colonial meeting. Leaders from every colony except Georgia met during September in Philadelphia for what is now called the First Continental Congress.

The Congress urged support for the people of Boston and condemned the Intolerable Acts. It demanded British laws that taxed colonists be repealed at once. It criticized the practice of keeping an army in the colonies and set up an organization to ban British imports.

In Massachusetts, the atmosphere was becoming tense. General Thomas Gage, who had replaced Thomas Hutchinson as governor, canceled a meeting of the Massachusetts Assembly, but the members met anyway. Local leaders organized militias and began to collect and store military supplies. Since Great Britain would not loosen its hold on the colonies, it seemed as if war was certain.

Parliament declared Massachusetts to be in a state of rebellion. It sent more redcoats to Gage in Boston and ordered him to arrest Patriot leaders. On the night of April 18, 1775, Gage sent 700 men under the command of Lieutenant Colonel Francis Smith to arrest Sam Adams and John Hancock in Lexington. Smith's troops were then to seize weapons and military supplies that the Patriots had been gathering in Concord.

Fortunately the Patriots were watching the British troops' movements closely. So when the

The First Continental Congress warned the colonies to arm themselves in case of attack. As a result, many communities created military groups called militias. Special groups were formed within each militia. These groups were made up of men who would be available to fight on a minute's notice. These soldiers were called Minutemen.

Paul Revere's ride

troops set out, Paul Revere and William Dawes, another Patriot, rode ahead and warned the colonists. First they rode to Lexington and warned Adams and Hancock. Then, joined by Samuel Prescott, they rode toward Lexington. Along the way, Revere and Dawes were captured by a British patrol, but Prescott escaped and was able to warn the people of Concord.

At dawn, British soldiers reached Lexington. Facing them on the town common were brave Patriots, a group of about 70 Minutemen ranging from teenagers to men in their sixties. The Minutemen were ready to give up their lives for freedom. And then a British soldier opened fire. It was "the shot heard round the world."

THREE

Sons of Violence

There is another side to this story. This side is based on the viewpoint of the Loyalists, or Tories, who supported Great Britain's right to rule and tax the colonies. In the opinion of these people, it was not the British who fired the first shot at Lexington that began the Revolutionary War. It was the people who called themselves Patriots, but who were really rebels, who started the war. The Loyalists believed themselves to be the true patriots, and colonial history can be used to support their viewpoint.

Countries established colonies to extend their power in the world. England had sent over, supported, and protected the people who came to America. It put a great deal of effort and expense into developing and maintaining its colonies, which were a part of Great Britain.

Each colony was supposed to be profitable. To help bring that about, Parliament passed laws to regulate, or control, trade into and out of the colonies. These laws stated that all goods being carried between Great Britain and its colonies had to pass through Great Britain and be carried by British or American ships with British or American crews. The purpose of these laws was not to punish the colonies but to help them contribute to Great Britain's economy. The laws together were known as the Acts of Trade and Navigation, and they operated quite well for more than a hundred years.

And then came war involving all the important powers in Europe. Known as the Seven Years' War, this conflict extended across the Atlantic to become the French and Indian War in North America. Great Britain poured money and manpower into the fight to protect and extend its territory.

With this increased investment came a renewed interest in the colonies by the British. Some colonists saw this interest as a threat to their liberties, but Great Britain was merely protecting its interest.

When the French and Indian War ended, the British won a victory, but they also had run up tremendous debt. The war had helped bring about a national debt of some 130 million pounds sterling. But that wasn't all. The debts would surely increase because 10,000 soldiers were needed to defend the territory they had recently won from the French.

> Fighting did not end with the British victory in the French and Indian War. In the summer of 1763, Native Americans, fearing that their land would be overrun by white settlers, began attacking and capturing colonial forts between Lake Superior and the lower Mississippi River. Since the colonists would not, or could not, protect themselves, the British had to help. In October, Parliament passed a proclamation that provided separate areas for Native American and colonial settlements. Despite the fairness of the proclamation, some colonists complained that Great Britain was interfering.

Who was going to pay for this? The colonists did not offer to pay, even though they would benefit greatly from this action.

It was not at all fair for the colonists to think that the British should have to pay the total cost for protecting the colonies. After all, the soldiers were protecting the colonists' lives and property. Besides, the citizens of Great Britain were already paying an average of 25 shillings a year in taxes compared to the colonists' average of sixpence a year. That was 50 times more!

The Sugar Act was nothing greatly new and different to the colonists. Parliament had already been involved in regulating trade. All this act did was add some duties, none of which were very high. In fact, the tax on molasses was actually lowered with passage of the Sugar Act. Yet the colonists complained.

Money raised from the Sugar Act was still not enough to take the heavy burden off the British people. Because of this, Parliament passed the Stamp

In New York, colonists burned stamps to protest the Stamp Act.

British tax stamp

Act in 1765. As with the Sugar Act, this law was not something greatly new or unfair to the colonists. The British had already been paying stamp taxes for a long time. Why shouldn't the colonists pay similar taxes? All the money raised would be used to pay the troops and the salaries of the officials in the American colonies. But again, colonists complained.

This time was different, though. This time they did not just complain. They formed secret organizations and called them the Sons of Liberty. They organized themselves and protested the actions of Great Britain in the name of liberty, but they did not

Tax officials were sometimes tarred and feathered.

★ ★ ★ ★ ★ ★ ★ ★ ★ ★ ★ ★ ★ ★ ★

In Boston, stamp distributor Andrew Oliver experienced the violence of the Sons of Liberty. Even before he had received stamps to sell, there were protests in Boston, and a likeness of himself was hanged and then burned. An angry mob tore down the building they thought would be his office. Then they moved to his house, where they ripped down his fence and threw rocks at his windows. Before the mob could break into the house to attack Oliver, the sheriff arrived on the scene.

The next day, representatives of the Sons of Liberty paid a visit to Oliver and warned him that if he didn't resign, his house would be destroyed and his life would be in danger. Fearing for his life, Oliver resigned.

stop there. They harassed neighbors who were Loyalists and terrorized people whose jobs required them to carry out the laws. Stamp officials as well as royal officials were attacked and sometimes tarred and feathered to force them to resign. To the many victims of their harsh methods, these groups were known as the Sons of Violence.

As the protests and violence spread through the colonies, it became clear that the Stamp Act would be impossible to enforce. The British Government would have to repeal the law. They would have to find another way to get the colonists to contribute money.

The Townshend Acts, the next taxes levied on the colonies, were passed to avoid taxing the colonists directly. Instead of collecting taxes at places of business, taxes were collected at the ports to which products were shipped. Although only a few products were taxed and this method had been used before, colonists resisted. Protests, riots, and a boycott followed. Customs officials were attacked and injured, and merchants who did not participate in the boycott were blacklisted.

Although the colonists who disagreed with the British were in the minority (one third were opposed, one third were loyal, and one third were neutral), they were a very vocal and active minority. When British officials in Boston seized the ship of patriot leader John Hancock, which was filled with smuggled goods, an angry mob formed and attacked the officials and their property. More troops were needed to restore order in Boston.

But additional troops in Boston seemed to make the rebel colonists even angrier. They taunted the soldiers and started street fights. With the growing climate of violence, the events of March 5 were not surprising. But it was not really a massacre, as the Patriots claimed. The Loyalists viewed it as a riot.

On the night of Monday, March 5, 1770, a gang of colonists began throwing snowballs and chunks of ice at a British soldier standing guard in front of the Customs House. When the crowd moved toward him, the soldier loaded his gun and called for help. His calls were heard at the main guardhouse, which was close by. Six privates and a corporal rushed across the street, pushed their way through the crowd, and formed a half-circle with their guns held in front of them. In a short time, Captain Thomas Preston, the officer in charge, joined them.

The soldiers pleaded with the crowd to move back, but the angry colonists would not listen. Instead, they shouted insults and hit the soldiers' muskets with sticks. And then a soldier was knocked down when a colonist hit him hard with a piece of wood. Fearing for his life, the soldier scrambled to his feet and fired his musket into the

The British soldiers who shot at colonists were tried for murder. They were defended in court by Josiah Quincy, Jr., and John Adams, Sam Adams's second cousin. Although John Adams spoke out against the Stamp Act, he was also opposed to violent protests.

All but two of the soldiers were found innocent by the jury. The two were not found guilty of murder but of manslaughter. Each of them had an M branded on his thumb and then was allowed to return to his unit.

John Adams

crowd. Within seconds, other soldiers fired, too, killing three colonists and wounding eight. Two of the wounded died later.

If the people who called themselves Patriots really were, they would have been supporting the laws that their country—Great Britain—had passed. They would not have been complaining or protesting. They certainly would not have been breaking the laws by destroying property and harming people.

When the Patriots dressed up as the Mohawk and dumped tea into Boston Harbor, it was another criminal act. Many people, including those who had been critical of the British, thought that this action went too far. So did the leaders of the British government. That's why they had to make consequences severe for those who committed criminal acts. They passed the Coercive Act, called the Intolerable Acts by the Patriots, to force the colonists to take responsibility for their actions. Why shouldn't the people of Boston have to pay for the tea their citizens had destroyed?

Protesting Patriots dumped tea into Boston Harbor.

The growing unrest and the increase in criminal acts had to be addressed. Colonists were meeting and organizing, even when it was against the law. General Thomas Gage, the governor of Massachusetts, became concerned and ordered arms and ammunition removed from some areas to protect them from the colonists. While making arrangements to raid a colonial supply of weapons and ammunition, Gage received a message from the Secretary of State for the colonies back in Great Britain. The message authorized him to take strong action against the colonists. It would be better to fight the rebels before they had a chance to get better organized.

But the rebels were much better organized than the British realized. The colonists knew that the British were starting a military operation and were able to warn the people in towns along the way. Because they were so well organized, colonists were armed and ready for the British when they got to Lexington on the morning of April 19, 1775.

As to who fired the first shot at Lexington, the rebels blamed the British, but Loyalists had a different opinion. Loyalists believed that the first shot was fired at British soldiers from a nearby tavern or from behind a stone wall beside it. After that the British soldiers began firing, too. Some say that orders were given to fire; others say that the soldiers began firing after being shot at. In any event the war between the British and the rebel colonists had begun.

FOUR

The Struggle for Freedom

Many people believe that the colonists who opposed British rule were the real Patriots. It was these people who risked their lives against all odds in the name of freedom and liberty. These people became the heroes once the fighting began.

After Lexington, the British troops moved on to Concord. There they destroyed some of the arms and ammunition stored by the colonists. Then the British began their march back to Boston.

But the sixteen-mile march was not easy. Patriots in the area had heard what had happened and were upset. Angered at reports that the British were ransacking homes and harming innocent people, more Patriots gathered to fight back. As the redcoats made their way back to Boston, Patriots fired at them every step of the way.

Although only 72 of the 2,000 British soldiers were killed on the march to Boston, something very important had happened for the colonists. When

The British, retreating from Concord, were fired on by small groups of Patriots.

trouble came, people throughout the countryside were willing to help. In fact, thousands of Patriots answered the call to duty. This showed how many people valued the cause of the Patriots in their struggle for freedom.

Most of the British soldiers got back to Boston, but they were not safe. Their actions had greatly aroused the colonists, and 20,000 Patriots gathered

36

across the Charles River at Cambridge. Meanwhile, men on horseback were carrying the news of Lexington and Concord to other colonies.

When Lord Dunmore, royal governor of Virginia, seized the colonial militia's supply of powder and ammunition, many people realized that problems with the British reached beyond Massachusetts. Problems were widespread and affected all colonists.

In Boston, Patriots organized their forces and surrounded the British. The Patriots had muskets and ammunition, but what they really needed were cannons so they could attack the British from a safe distance. Fortunately, other brave Patriots would soon help them get what they needed.

Ethan Allen and his Green Mountain Boys, from the area that is now Vermont, joined forces with troops sponsored by Massachusetts and commanded by Benedict Arnold. In the early morning hours of May 10, they attacked Fort Ticonderoga on the shore of Lake Champlain, surprising the sleeping British soldiers. While the crumbling fort was of little value to the victors, the 80 cannons along with powder and ammunition were a great prize.

Meanwhile, in Philadelphia, the Second Continental Congress was meeting. All 13 colonies were represented this time. Some of the most important men in America were delegates, including Sam

Adams, John Adams, John Hancock, Benjamin Franklin, Patrick Henry, George Washington, and Thomas Jefferson. The delegates decided it was time for all the colonies to get involved in the conflict with Great Britain. They agreed to organize an army and chose George Washington to be the commander in chief because of his military experience as well as his good judgment and sense of responsibility.

George Washington with his troops

Before the Continental Army could be properly organized, the conflict continued in Boston. The plan of the Patriots was to occupy the high points surrounding the city so that gunmen could shoot at enemy forces below. Of the two hills—Bunker Hill and Breed's Hill—they decided to take Breed's Hill, since it was closer to Boston. After the Patriots took the hill, they were attacked by the British. The

The Battle of Bunker Hill

Patriots fought off the two assaults but could not hold off the third. The British won the battle, which became known as the battle of Bunker Hill, but at a heavy cost. Of the 2,300 British soldiers, the number listed as killed or wounded was 1,054. The Patriots lost the battle but gained volunteers after word spread of their courage under fire.

Despite the fighting taking place between the American colonists and the British, many people hoped the conflict could be settled peacefully. Delegates to the Second Continental Congress adopted the Olive Branch Petition on July 5, 1775. This petition was a plea for the British government to address the concerns of the colonists. King George III, however, would not even read the petition. Soon after hearing his refusal, the delegates wrote another document. This one, called "A Declaration of the Causes and Necessity of Taking Up Arms," announced that the colonists were willing to fight for their freedom.

Fighting for freedom, however, was easier said than done. After all, the colonists would be fighting against the most powerful nation on earth. Great Britain had a population of 8 million from which to build its army. The British had experienced, well-trained generals to command their forces. They had factories to make weapons and a powerful navy.

The colonies, on the other hand, had only about 2 million people, 500,000 of whom were slaves and would not be allowed to fight. They had few experienced officers to command their troops, no navy, and very little money for weapons and supplies. What they did have was a strong desire to stop Great Britain from treating them unfairly. General Washington used that desire to help organize and train his army.

Washington's first victory came in Boston in the spring of 1776. During the winter, Colonel Henry Knox and his men had used teams of oxen and sleds to haul captured cannons and guns from Fort Ticon-

Colonel Henry Knox directed his men to haul captured British artillery from Fort Ticonderoga to Boston.

deroga to Boston. Washington ordered the weapons pulled up Dorchester Heights, south of Boston. From there they would easily be able to hit British troops below.

General Howe, commander of the British forces, realized his troops did not have a chance against the new weapons. So on March 17, 1776, Howe ordered all 4,000 of his men out of Boston. They sailed to a British naval base in Nova Scotia. It was a great victory for the Patriots.

For the first time in many years, there were no British troops in the colonies. But that would not last for long. The British had no intention of giving the colonists their freedom. And as more colonists were killed in the conflict, more and more Patriots would settle for nothing less than freedom.

It wasn't long before everyone in the colonies was talking about independence. By June 1776 the members of the Second Continental Congress were ready to act. On June 7, Richard Henry Lee of Virginia introduced a resolution stating that the

★ ★ ★ ★ ★ ★ ★ ★ ★ ★ ★ ★ ★ ★ ★

One of the most important voices in getting colonists to think about independence from Great Britain was Thomas Paine. Paine, born in England, had not been in America long before he wrote a pamphlet called *Common Sense*. In it he attacked King George III, as well as the British form of government. He stated that people have a natural right to rule themselves, and he urged the colonists to declare their independence and create their own nation.

colonies were free and independent states. Before voting on the resolution, Congress appointed a committee to write a statement explaining why they were declaring their independence from Great Britain.

John Adams was appointed to the committee. So were Benjamin Franklin, Robert Livingston of New York, and Roger Sherman of Connecticut. But it was another member of the committee, 33-year-old Thomas Jefferson, who wrote most of the document that became known as the Declaration of Independence.

Congress met on July 1 to consider the Declaration of Independence. For three days they discussed and debated every point. Finally, on July 4, 1776, Congress adopted the Declaration of Independence. It officially ended British rule over the colonies and began a new nation—the United States of America. Fifty-six delegates from the 13 colonies signed their names to the document. Signing the Declaration of Independence took a great deal of courage. By putting their names on this document, these men were becoming traitors in the eyes of the British. The punishment for being a traitor was death.

The British had no intention of accepting the Declaration of Independence. They were determined to keep a tight grip on the colonies, and they were prepared to use military force to do so. The

The Declaration of Independence was one of the most important and influential political documents ever written. It stated that all men were created equal and that they have God-given rights to life, liberty, and the pursuit of happiness. Governments are created to make sure these rights are available, and if they fail to do so, then the people have the right to get rid of the government.

The Declaration of Independence also contains specific charges against King George III. Twenty-six separate crimes that the king committed were listed.

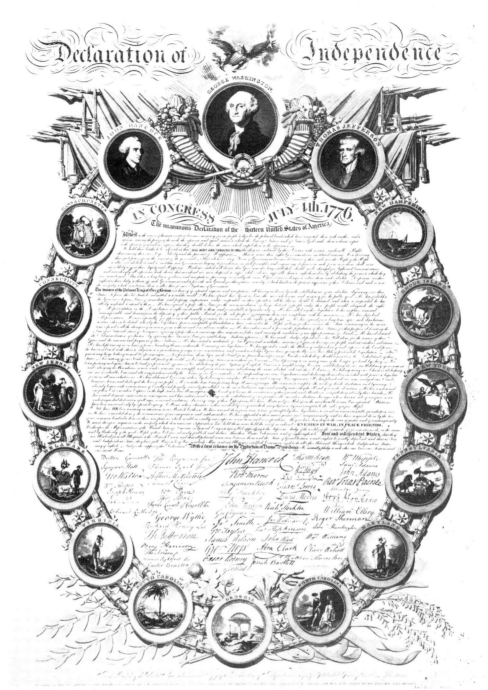

The Declaration of Independence

British hired German soldiers called Hessians to help them fight. This combined force captured New York City in September 1776. Loyalists cheered the British victory and then attacked their Patriot neighbors. When a fire broke out on September 21, Patriots were blamed. Suspects were rounded up, and without even a trial some were hanged and others were thrown into the fire.

After several more defeats it looked as if the end was near for the Continental Army and for the United States of America. But then on Christmas night, 1776, Washington led his 2,400 men across the Delaware River to surprise the Hessian troops in

Washington and his troops crossing the Delaware

Trenton. About 25 Hessians were killed, 90 wounded, and 900 taken prisoner. On January 3, 1777, Washington's troops went on to capture Princeton from the British. These victories brought new hope to the Patriot cause and helped bring new volunteers to the army.

The turning point of the war came when British General John Burgoyne tried to move his army from Canada to New York. As Burgoyne's troops marched south, the colonial army's numbers swelled as local citizens joined to protect their homes and property. By the time Burgoyne reached Saratoga, New York, he was completely surrounded by the army of General Horatio Gates. Burgoyne had no choice but to surrender his 5,000 men.

Saratoga was a great victory for the Patriots, especially since it helped convince France to help the United States openly against Great Britain. Still, more battles were fought, and more hardships were suffered. Washington's army spent the winter of 1777–1778 at Valley Forge, Pennsylvania. It was a long, cold winter, and both food and clothing were very scarce. Many soldiers deserted; thousands more died of cold, disease, and starvation.

Great Britain's last efforts were aimed at the southern colonies, where they hoped they could get more Loyalist support. They won several battles, but they were continually opposed by small groups of

France had been providing the Patriots with guns, ammunition, and clothing since early in the war, but this aid was given secretly to avoid another war with their bitter enemy. After Saratoga, when it appeared that Great Britain would be defeated, the French provided troops and ships. One ship was given to Captain John Paul Jones, who used it to fight against the powerful British navy. Jones's victories shocked the world and encouraged the Patriots.

Nancy Hart defending her home against Tories

★ ★ ★ ★ ★ ★ ★ ★ ★ ★ ★ ★ ★ ★

Men were not the only Patriots during the Revolutionary War. Women supported the cause of liberty by raising money, collecting supplies, boycotting British goods, defending their homes, and helping during battles. When six Tories raided her family cabin in Georgia, Nancy Hart grabbed her musket. She killed one raider, wounded another, and captured the rest. During the battle of Monmouth, in New Jersey, Mary Ludwig Hays earned the nickname Molly Pitcher for carrying pitchers of water to the thirsty soldiers. When her husband, an artillery gunner, collapsed in the blistering heat, she reportedly took his place loading a cannon until the battle was won.

guerilla fighters who were difficult to defeat or capture. When Great Britain's Lord Cornwallis moved into Virginia, he was met by American and French troops. After more than a week of shelling, Cornwallis, unable to escape, was ready to surrender.

At long last the war was near an end. The colonists who opposed the British fought for their freedom against tremendous odds. Many believe that these heroic people were the true patriots of the American Revolution.

FIVE

The Struggle for Order

For the Loyalists the war was not a struggle for freedom. Instead, it was a struggle for order. The demands of the rebels were unreasonable, and their methods were unacceptable. In siding with Great Britain, the Loyalists were supporting a country's right to govern its people.

When the war began, the views of the rebels did not accurately represent the views of the majority of Americans. In 1775, most of the colonists did not want to take part in a rebellion. They wanted to go about their everyday lives, working and raising their families. They had to be convinced that this war was worth fighting. But the rebel leaders were up to this challenge. They persuaded many colonists to believe that they had to fight for their freedom.

How were the leaders able to convince so many colonists to risk their lives by going to war? They used exaggeration skillfully. They exaggerated every account of the conflict between themselves and the British. The rebel leaders realized that the war was not just against Great Britain; it was a war for the minds of the colonists.

When British forces returned to Boston after fighting in Lexington and Concord, exaggerated accounts of their behavior caused many colonists to join the rebel forces. Express riders carried the news to all the colonies. One account, signed by Dr. Joseph Warren, told of pregnant women being driven into the streets and old men being shot in their homes. Warren wrote, "The barbarous murders committed on our innocent brethren on Wednesday the 19th instant have made it absolutely necessary that we immediately raise an army to defend our wives and children from the butchering hands of an inhuman soldiery . . . ."

What the news did not tell was that the British were retreating and doing their best to defend themselves against the angry colonists. The accounts also did not mention the cruel and brutal acts committed by the rebels. Lord Percy, a British officer, reported that wounded British soldiers who fell into the hands of the rebels were scalped and had their ears cut off in a few cases.

General Gage issued his own account of the incidents, but he was too late. Many people throughout the colonies had already made up their minds,

General Gage

although the information was inaccurate. Even some of the royal governors were upset at the accounts that were spread by the rebels. Governor Jonathan Trumbull of Connecticut wrote Gage a letter accusing him of unfairly attacking the colonists and of disgraceful behavior.

★ ★ ★ ★ ★ ★ ★ ★ ★ ★ ★ ★ ★ ★ ★

By June 1 an account of the events at Lexington and Concord had reached Great Britain. But like the other early accounts, this one came from the rebels. The Massachusetts Provincial Congress had hired Captain John Derby to sail to Great Britain with the rebel account of the action. Derby beat the slower British ship and distributed his account to the newspapers, which quickly printed it. The first news story charged the British troops with shooting down the unharmed, the aged and infirm as well as killing the wounded and "mangling their bodies in a most shocking manner." Readers were outraged.

Gage denied the charges but could not convince Trumbull of his innocence. Connecticut, in an effort to punish Gage's troops, stopped sending supplies to Boston. So did Rhode Island, New York, and Pennsylvania.

Despite the exaggerated reports, many colonists continued to support Great Britain. But supporting Great Britain was becoming more and more difficult. Rebel groups made threats on the Loyalists' lives and property. Some were beaten, tarred and feathered, or branded with a *T* for Tory. In Montreal a representative of the Massachusetts Provincial Congress warned merchants that if they helped the British in Boston, rebels would destroy their city.

Still, Loyalists helped fight the rebels. In Virginia, loyal colonists joined with freed slaves and British soldiers to fight against rebels. When rebel forces were sent into Canada, Loyalists joined the

British to protect their towns. They held off the rebels at Quebec and helped capture rebel leader Ethan Allen at Montreal.

Things did not go so well in Boston. Even though the British had claimed victory at Bunker Hill, their losses had been great. General Gage was relieved from his command and replaced by Lieutenant General William Howe. Hopelessly surrounded, Howe knew the British had no choice but to withdraw from Boston. The Loyalists, knowing that they would be punished by the rebels, knew they had to leave also. When the British left Boston on March 16, 1776, nearly 1,500 Loyalists sailed with them.

General Howe evacuating Boston

With the Declaration of Independence came the realization by the British that the colonists would have to be forced to remain a part of the British empire. It also brought about questions by stating that "all men are created equal," but not mentioning how this was so. Were they equal in size, strength, or abilities? Everyone knew that was not the case. So how exactly were they equal? And if all men are created equal, why did many of the rebels own slaves? How could these people call for liberty and yet deny liberty to fellow human beings?

The Declaration of Independence may have been confusing and even less than honest, but it had a tremendous effect on the way Loyalists were treated. No longer were these people seen as citizens having viewpoints different from those of the rebels. Cooperating with the British was helping the enemy. That is treason, which is punishable by death. Congress declared it illegal to help the British in any way or even to speak against opposing Great Britain.

In New York, people believed to be Loyalists were in constant danger. So many were arrested that special committees had to be created to carry out the punishments. Life was no easier for those not arrested. Angry crowds attacked Loyalists, ransacking their homes and running many of them out of town.

Angry crowds of Patriots harrassed Loyalists in various ways.

When General Howe's British troops landed on Long Island, hundreds of Loyalists stood on the beach and welcomed them. So many volunteered to fight that Howe established an American unit. The Loyalists became valuable members of the fighting force because they were familiar with the rugged country over which they would have to fight.

The burning of New York

With the help of Loyalists, the British campaign in New York was a huge success. First they attacked Long Island, losing only about 400 men compared to the rebel losses of more than 1,000. Washington

Soon after the British captured New York, a fire broke out. Warnings about the fire could not be given because the church bells had been melted down for ammunition. Firefighting equipment could not be found. As a result the blaze swept through the city, destroying nearly 500 buildings. Believed to be caused by rebels, the fire left most of the city in ashes. It was a setback for Howe, who was planning to use the houses as winter quarters for his men.

saved his army from total defeat by retreating across the East River to Manhattan Island.

After delaying for several weeks, Howe followed Washington and drove his army north. Following more defeats, Washington's forces withdrew across the Hudson River to New Jersey. His army of more than 10,000 now numbered less than 3,000. The Continental Army was very close to defeat.

The British made a plan to defeat the rebels. General George Clinton, with a small force, would hold New York. General Howe would take 15,000 men on 260 ships south to the Chesapeake Bay. From there they would march north and capture Philadelphia. Then they would continue north and meet General Burgoyne, who was leading an invasion force from Canada, in Albany, New York.

The plan partially worked. Clinton held New York as Howe defeated the rebel army in several battles before taking Philadelphia. But Burgoyne was having trouble in the north, and Howe was unable to break out of Philadelphia to help him.

As Burgoyne moved south from Canada, he headed toward Albany. Some believed he should have moved his troops by boat along Lake George and the upper Hudson River, but Burgoyne chose the land route instead. He had heard that they would be joined by hundreds of Loyalists ready to fight for the king and Great Britain. Two or three hundred men did join the British, but many did not have weapons and most had no military training. More Loyalists might have joined, but many were frightened at the thought of being caught and punished as traitors by the rebels.

Burgoyne's march toward Albany was difficult. Roads had to be cleared of trees that had been cut by retreating rebels. Native Americans who had volunteered to help the British would not follow orders and attacked innocent women and children, angering the colonists. By the time Burgoyne reached Saratoga, he was surrounded and had no chance of escaping.

For British supporters, Burgoyne's loss at Saratoga was more than a bitter defeat. It was the beginning of the end of their struggle to bring order to the American colonies. The French were ready to enter the fighting, and they were actually concerned that the war might be settled before they could get involved and fight against their rival. They quickly made an alliance with the United States and began sending men and ships to help the colonists. In time, Holland and Spain—other enemies of the British, began sending aid, too.

The alliance with France angered many British supporters. How could the rebels be allies of France? It wasn't that long ago that the colonists were fighting alongside the British against the French. Besides, the French government treated its citizens much more unfairly than the British did. How could the French possibly be fighting for liberty?

With France in the war, the British had to fight against a larger army and a more powerful navy. There were other problems, too. Great Britain had to protect its colonies in other parts of the world as well as protect itself from attack.

British soldiers desperately needed help from the American colonists. Many believed that if the army focused its efforts in the southern colonies, there would be more Loyalist support. But again the British overestimated.

Despite the lack of support, the southern plan worked for a while. Using the navy effectively, the British captured Savannah, Georgia, and Charleston,

The rebels successfully withstood a British attack at Fort Sullivan in South Carolina.

South Carolina. Then Cornwallis defeated Gates at Camden, South Carolina. But soon the rebels began using hit-and-run tactics with successful results. It wasn't long before most of the South was controlled by the rebels.

Cornwallis marched his army north into Virginia, looking for a decisive victory. What he found, however, was Washington's army united with French forces. He was heavily outnumbered. Offshore was a French fleet preventing him from getting help or supplies. Cornwallis was trapped! Yorktown would be the last major battle of the war.

Who were the brave Loyalists who risked their lives to serve the king and their country? They were a variety of people. They were freed slaves and Native Americans. They were colonists from every social class and from all walks of life: coopers (barrel or cask makers), laborers, merchants, mariners, professional men, and tradespeople.

Loyalists were ridiculed, beaten, jailed, and even killed because of their beliefs. Some had their property seized and were forced to leave town. Others left on their own. By the end of the war, it is believed that up to 100,000 Loyalists left the colonies to live somewhere else.

Many, however, chose to stay and fight for their beliefs. During the course of the war, as many as 40 regiments were organized, including the Royal

Some of the Loyalists came from famous families. William Franklin, son of Benjamin, was the governor of New Jersey as well as the head of the Board of American Loyalists. Peggy Shippen, from a prominent Loyalist family in Pennsylvania, married Benedict Arnold. After this, his political sympathies began to change.

Greens, the Roman Catholic Volunteers, the Black Volunteers, and Butler's Rangers. Many died in the service of their country.

In some minds, it was the Loyalists, the people who remained true to their country, who were the heroes of the war. It was the Loyalists who were the true patriots of the American Revolution.

SIX

What Do You Think?

Yorktown was the last major battle of the American Revolution, but it was not the end of the war. Skirmishes between the Americans and the British were fought in several colonies, especially on the western frontier. Great Britain continued to fight France and Spain in other parts of the world.

It took more than a month for word of the British defeat at Yorktown to reach Great Britain. Lord North, the prime minister, was reported to have taken the news as he would "a musket ball in the chest." King George III was shocked but optimistic. He was ready to continue the war until the British won.

Meanwhile, George Washington was cautious. While impressed with the victory at Yorktown, he was not convinced the war was over, especially since the British did not withdraw their forces. So Washington made plans for 1782. He planned to attack Charleston and New York. He also planned to meet new British attacks. But the attacks did not come.

New leaders were taking over in Great Britain, and these leaders were interested in ending the war. As a result, peace negotiations between Great Britain and the United States began in Paris in April 1782. Richard Oswald was the chief British delegate. Benjamin Franklin represented the United States. Later he was joined by John Adams, John Jay, and Henry Laurens.

At first, negotiations went slowly because France and Spain were still at war with Great Britain, and each new battle changed the way the countries viewed peace. So representatives from Great Britain and the United States decided to work on a separate peace agreement, which they completed on November 30, 1782. In this preliminary peace agreement, Great Britain agreed to

★ ★ ★ ★ ★ ★ ★ ★ ★ ★ ★ ★ ★ ★ ★

The time between the surrender of Yorktown and the signing of the final treaty with Great Britain was a challenging time for George Washington. He could not disband his army because he was not certain of peace. His troops, who had not been paid because Congress lacked the money, were growing restless and angry. Some officers, thinking that Congress would ignore its promise to them after their years of hard service, threatened to revolt. Washington met with them and convinced them to be patient and demonstrate their confidence in Congress.

It was a confusing time because it was not certain how this new nation—the United States—would be ruled. Some suggested to Washington that he use the power of his position as commander in chief to make himself the king of the United States. Washington angrily refused.

This unfinished painting by Benjamin West shows John Hay, John Adams, Benjamin Franklin, and Henry Laurens at the signing of the Treaty of Paris on September 3, 1783.

accept the United States as an independent nation with boundaries from the Atlantic to the Mississippi, from Florida (now owned by Spain) to Canada. Great Britain would remove its soldiers from the United States, and the Americans would not punish the Loyalists. The agreement would take effect when Great Britain reached an agreement with its other enemies.

It took about six more months before Great Britain came to terms with France and Spain. A peace agreement was created and signed in Paris on September 3, 1783. After eight long years the war

Disbanding the Continental Army at New Windsor, New York, on November 3, 1783

between the United States and Great Britain was officially over.

The Revolutionary War was costly to both sides. Great Britain spent more than $700 million and the United States more than $500 million to fight the war. Both sides lost warships and hundreds of merchant ships. Thousands of men died from wounds or disease during the conflict.

Still, Americans gained a lot from the Revolutionary War. They gained their independence, a vast amount of land, the right to trade with whomever they wanted, and the right to govern themselves

★ ★ ★ ★ ★ ★ ★ ★ ★ ★ ★ ★ ★ ★ ★

Congress did not have the power to tax, so to pay for the war they printed their own money. Called Continentals, these bills were the first paper money that could be used in all the colonies. Paul Revere engraved the plates from which these bills were printed.

Congress issued about $200 million in continental money. By the end of the war, the money was worthless because so much had been issued and because it could not be backed up with gold or silver. "Not worth a Continental" became a popular phrase in America.

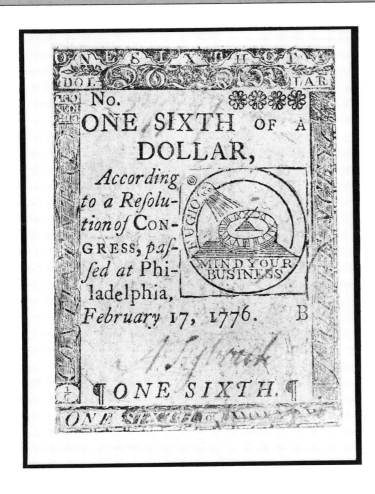

Colonial currency

without British interference. But the words that were written in the Declaration of Independence were not completely followed. Millions of blacks remained slaves. Women did not have the same rights as men, nor did the poor. Native Americans had to continue to fight for the territory that was theirs.

After the war the next challenge for the United States of America was to form a government. Colonial governments had to be changed into state governments, independent from Great Britain. The new nation also had to create a central government to deal with issues common to the states. Constitutions had to be written to replace colonial charters, and state legislatures had to be formed to replace colonial assemblies.

Much discussion and debate took place before agreements were reached regarding the new government. It took until 1789 before the new system of government was ready to begin. On April 30, at the corner of Broad and Wall streets in New York City, George Washington was sworn in as the first president of the United States.

The Revolutionary War was the first modern revolution against a monarchy and an empire, but it would not be the last. In 1789 a revolution took place in France. In the nineteenth century many countries in western Europe and Latin America

Washington's entry into New York, November 1783

tried to change their governments to be like the one created by the United States. In the twentieth century, countries in Asia and Africa have tried to do the same thing.

So who were the real patriots of the Revolutionary War? Were they the people who opposed the British and fought against them? Or were they the people who remained loyal to Great Britain?

Those who believe that the real patriots of the Revolutionary War were the colonists who opposed the British make several points to support their view.

1. British rule of the colonies was unfair and unjust.

2. Colonists were fighting for liberty and freedom.

3. Colonists faced tremendous odds.

4. They risked their lives and property in opposing the British.

People who believe that the real patriots of the Revolutionary War were the colonists who remained loyal to Great Britain use these points to support their position.

1. Great Britain had the right to govern the colonies and to levy taxes.

2. These colonists were following the law.

3. They were being loyal and supportive of their country.

4. They risked their lives and property in opposing the rebels.

Which side is correct? Could both sides be right? Or could both be wrong? You have read about both sides of the issue. Now consider each one carefully. What do you think?

★ ★ ★   # Time Line   ★ ★ ★

Mid-1700s Great Britain possesses 13 colonies in North America

1760 George III becomes the ruler of Great Britain

1763 Great Britain wins the French and Indian War

1764 Parliament passes the Sugar Act to raise money in the colonies

1765 **March** Parliament passes the Stamp Act

May Colonists create the Sons of Liberty to fight the Stamp Act; Virginia's House of Burgesses passes the Virginia Resolves

October Colonial representatives pass the Declaration of Rights and Grievances

1767 Parliament passes the Townshend Acts

1770 British soldiers fire at a crowd of Boston citizens

1773 **May** Parliament passes the Tea Act

December Boston Tea Party takes place

1774 Parliament passes a series of laws to force Massachusetts to pay for the dumped tea

September The First Continental Congress meets in Philadelphia

1775 **April** Colonists and British soldiers exchange shots at Lexington; the war begins

May The Second Continental Congress meets in Philadelphia; Washington is appointed commander in chief

June British win the battle of Bunker Hill

1776 **July** Congress adopts the Declaration of Independence; Howe captures New York for the British

December Washington surprises Hessian troops at Trenton

1777 British are defeated at Saratoga

1778   France declares war on Great Britain

1780   British capture Charleston but do not get colonial support

1781   Cornwallis surrenders British forces at Yorktown

1782   Peace treaty is written; Great Britain agrees to accept the United States as an independent nation

1783   Treaty of Paris is signed; the war is officially over

★ ★ ★ Glossary ★ ★ ★

alliance—A union between nations

assembly—A group of elected people who made decisions for the colony; legislature

charter—The document that listed the colonists' rights and privileges

congress—A formal meeting for the discussion of problems

Congress—The legislature of the United States

cooper—A person who makes or repairs barrels or casks

correspond—To communicate by letter

duty—Tax

earthwork—A bank or wall of piled-up dirt used for defense

Hessians—German soldiers hired by the British

Loyalists—American colonists who supported Great Britain; Tories

manslaughter—The unlawful killing of someone without deliberate planning

monarchy—A government ruled by a king

monopoly—Exclusive control

mortar—A short-barreled cannon used to shoot shells in a high arc

negotiations—Process of discussing or bargaining to make an agreement

Parliament—The lawmaking body of Great Britain

petition—A formal document containing a request

proclamation—An official announcement

rebel—One who is in armed resistance to the established government

repeal—To cancel or take back

resolution—A formal statement of a decision put before or adopted by an assembly

skirmish—A brief fight between groups

Tories—American colonists who supported Great Britain; Loyalists

traitor—One who betrays his or her country

★ **For Further Reading** ★

If you would like to know more about the colonists before and during the Revolutionary War, here are some books that were helpful in writing *The Real Patriots of the American Revolution.*

Carter, Alden. *The American Revolution.* New York: Watts, 1992.

Foley, Paul. *Fresh Views of the American Revolution.* New York: Rizzoli, 1976.

Hibbert, Christopher. *Redcoats and Rebels.* New York: W. W. Norton, 1990.

Ketchum, Richard, ed. *The American Heritage Book of the Revolution.* New York: American Heritage, 1958.

Leckie, Robert. *The World Turned Upside Down.* New York: G.P. Putnam's Sons, 1973.

McDowell, Bart. *The Revolutionary War.* Washington: National Geographic, 1967.

Meltzer, Milton. *The American Revolutionaries.* New York: Crowell, 1987.

Nordstrom, Judy. *Concord and Lexington.* New York: Dillon, 1993.

Smith, Carter. *A Sourcebook on Colonial America: Governing and Teaching.* Brookfield, CT: Millbrook, 1991.

A Sourcebook on Colonial America: The Revolutionary War. Brookfield, CT: Millbrook, 1991.

For fiction that is set during the American Revolution, you might enjoy reading the following books.

Avi. *The Fighting Ground.* New York: J.B. Lippincott, 1984.

Brady, Esther Wood. *Tolver's Secret.* New York: Crown, 1976.

Collier, James Lincoln, and Christopher Collier. *My Brother Sam Is Dead.* New York: Scholastic, 1974.

Forbes, Esther. *Johnny Tremain.* Cambridge: Houghton Mifflin, 1943.

O'Dell, Scott. *Sarah Bishop.* New York: Scholastic, 1980.

★ ★ ★ ★ Index ★ ★ ★ ★

★ ★ About the Author ★ ★

Robert Young has been fascinated with the past ever since he walked through the house in which George Washington once lived. Besides writing books that help bring history alive, Robert job-shares a teaching position and visits schools to speak about writing. The author of 12 books for children and teachers, Robert lives in Eugene, Oregon, with his wife, Sara, and their son, Tyler.